CW00447909

purses
BAGS & MORE™

Designs by Pearl Louise Krush

HOUSE of
WHITE
BIRCHES

PUBLISHERS
SINCE 1947

Table of Contents

Ragtime Blues,
page 30

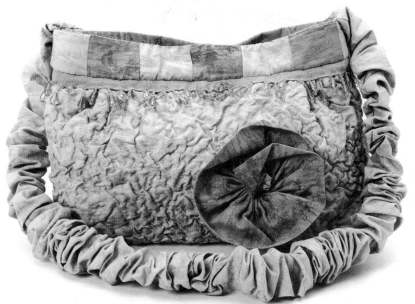

Puttin' On the Ritz,
page 4

On the Go, page 42

Purse & Bag Sewing Basics

Creating purses and bags requires a wide assortment of supplies and simple instructions. Read through the basics before you select your fabrics and other products to make the delightful variety of purses and bags presented in this book.

Fabric

Use high-quality fabrics such as 100-percent cotton fabrics from your local quilt or sewing store. If you don't have access to a local shop, there are many online stores that sell quality fabrics. All of the bags and purses in this book were made with 100-percent cotton fabrics.

Create your own styles by choosing prints and colors that appeal to you. The fabric market has an endless assortment of fabrics that are fully coordinated with large and small prints, tone-on-tone prints, directional prints and the always favorite stripes, checks, plaids and dots.

Pre-washing the fabric is not required. If you are concerned about colorfastness, place a two-inch strip of fabric into a bowl of very hot water to see if any dye releases. If the fabric bleeds, pre-wash the fabric before cutting out each project. Should the fabric bleed after being washed several times, eliminate the fabric. You don't want fabrics that bleed to be used for a purse or bag that may become wet.

Batting

Batting comes in a variety of weights and material choices such as polyester, cotton and wool. The bags in this book all used 100-percent cotton batting. Cotton batting does not provide a lot of bulk and it gives your project a nice, lightweight feel.

Buttons & Embellishments

Embellishments are a matter of choice. Your preference of fabrics and colors will determine the look of your bag or purse. Shop for creative beads, buttons, trims and closures to add to your bags and purses; you may even find unique items around your house that you can use to add your own personal touch.

Note: Many of the purse and bag designs in this book are created with quilted fabric. Cut, layer and quilt your fabrics as desired.

*Gathered Go-Go Purse, **page 37***

Puttin' On the Ritz

Add texture to any fabric for magical results. Top it off with a string of bling, and you're ready for a night on the town sporting a designer exclusive.

Finished Size
10 x 14 x 3 inches

Materials
- 44/45-inch-wide 100-percent cotton fabrics:
  - 1½ yards mottled green
  - ⅝ yard mottled orange
- 1 yard Texture Magic™ steam-activated shrinking fabric
- 1 yard green bead home-decorating trim
- 1 magnetic purse snap
- Pressing sheet
- Basic sewing supplies and equipment

Cutting

From mottled green:
- Cut one 24 x 30-inch rectangle.

- Cut one 14½-inch x fabric width strip. Subcut strip into one 14½ x 18-inch rectangle for lining, and two 5½ x 10½-inch rectangles for lining pockets.

- Cut one 2½-inch x fabric width strip. Subcut strip into seven 1½ x 2½-inch rectangles for bag band.

- Cut two 4½-inch x fabric width strips for handle.

From mottled orange:
- Cut one 6-inch x fabric width strip. Subcut strip into one 6 x 22-inch rectangle for flower, and two 5½ x 10½-inch rectangles for lining pockets.

- Cut one 2½-inch x fabric width strip. Subcut strip into seven 1½ x 2½-inch rectangles for bag band.

- Cut one 2-inch x fabric width strip. Subcut strip into two 14½-inch strips for lining bands.

- Cut one 5-inch x fabric strip for handle.

From Texture Magic:
- Cut one 24 x 30-inch rectangle.

Assembly
Sew right sides together using ¼-inch seam allowances unless otherwise indicated.

Fabric Texturing
1. Pin 24 x 30-inch Texture Magic rectangle to wrong side of 24 x 30-inch mottled green rectangle. Sew fabrics together with an overall meandering pattern.

2. Following manufacturer's instructions, remove pins and apply steam to texture fabric. *Do not touch Texture Magic fabric with iron.* Use pressing sheet when pressing during construction.

3. Trim textured fabric to 14½ x 18 inches.

Bag Body
1. Sew 1½ x 2½-inch mottled green and orange rectangles together along 1½-inch edges alternately to create bag band. Make two sets of seven rectangles, one beginning with mottled orange and one with mottled green, referring to Figure 1.

Figure 1

2. Mark center of 18-inch length of the 14½ x 18-inch textured rectangle.

3. Sew a band to each 14½-inch edge of textured rectangle. Lightly press the seam allowances toward band using caution to avoid the textured fabric piece.

4. Fold textured rectangle in half along marked center, right sides together. Sew side seams, matching raw edges and band seams. Lightly press side seams open.

5. Match side seam to center mark and pin 1½ inches from corner point. Double-stitch across corner to form box end. Trim to ½-inch seam allowance (Figure 2). Repeat on remaining side seam. Turn right side out.

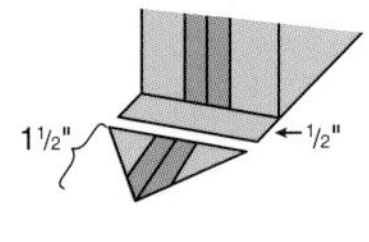

1½"   ½"

Figure 2

Bag Lining

1. Sew one 5½ x 10½-inch mottled green lining pocket to one 5½ x 10½-inch mottled orange lining pocket around all edges, leaving a 3-inch opening in one long edge for turning.

2. Trim corners and turn right side out. Press seams flat, turning opening edges to inside. Edgestitch long edge with the opening. Repeat to make two lining pockets.

3. Fold 14½ x 18-inch mottled green lining rectangle widthwise to mark center of 18-inch length; press. Position and pin pockets 2 inches from center and sides of lining, referring to Figure 3.

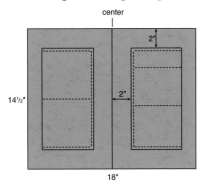

Figure 3

4. Edgestitch around sides and bottoms of pockets. If desired, stitch pockets into two or three sections, again referring to Figure 3.

5. Sew one 2 x 14½-inch mottled orange strip to each 14½-inch end of lining rectangle. Press seams toward bands.

6. Follow manufacturer's instructions to attach magnetic purse snap centered on right sides of lining bands.

7. Fold lining in half, right sides together, matching and pinning raw edges and band seams. Sew side seams together leaving a 3-inch opening in one side for turning.

8. Make box ends in lining referring to step 5 of Bag Body and Figure 2. *Do not turn right side out.*

Handles

1. Fold 5-inch x fabric width mottled orange strip in half lengthwise, right sides together. Sew together along length. Turn right side out and trim to 35 inches.

2. Sew two 4½-inch x fabric width mottled green strips together at short ends to make one long strip. Fold in half lengthwise, right sides together and sew. Turn right side out.

3. Insert the mottled orange strip into the long green strip, matching and pinning ends together. Sew across ends. Gather green strip evenly on orange strip creating a gathered handle.

4. Smooth gathers away from handle ends. Pin 3 inches from each end to hold back gathers.

Completing Bag

1. Pin handle ends to right side of bag centered over side seams and extending 2 inches beyond band edge (Figure 4). Baste handle ends in place. Remove pins.

Figure 4

2. Slide bag body into lining with right sides together. Match side seams and band raw edges. Sew around bag top, double-stitching across handle ends.

3. Turn right side out through opening in lining. Hand- or machine-stitch opening closed. Slip lining into bag, pulling handle up.

4. Press bands away from body and lining. Press top edge flat. Pin all layers together at band/body seam and edgestitch band/body seam (Figure 5).

Figure 5

5. Hand- or machine-stitch green bead home-decorating trim to right side of bag at band seam, overlapping ends at side seam (Figure 6).

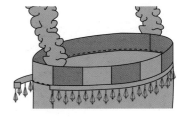

Figure 6

2. Hand-sew a gathering stitch ½ inch from pressed seam along length (Figure 7).

Figure 7

3. Pull gathering tight. Roll strip, with sewn end at center, to form large flower. Adjust gathering if necessary.

4. Tie ends of gathering thread to secure and tack strip ends to flower center.

5. Referring to photo, hand-stitch flower to bag front. ❖

Making the Flower

1. Fold the 6 x 22-inch mottled orange rectangle in half lengthwise with right sides together. Sew one end and length. Turn right side out. Press seam only flat.

On the Town

You can't go wrong with this little bag and its always fashionable color scheme. Make it dressy or casual with your fabric choices.

Finished Size
12 x 6 x 4 inches

Materials
- 44/45-inch-wide 100-percent cotton fabrics:
  - ⅝ yard black/cream polka dot
  - ½ yard red print
  - ¼ yard black print
- ⅝ yard thin cotton batting
- 4 (1-inch) black buttons
- 2 (⅝-inch) black buttons
- Cream thread for quilting
- Basting adhesive spray
- Basic sewing supplies and equipment

Cutting

From black/cream polka dot:
- Cut two 2½-inch x fabric width strips for patchwork.

- Cut four 2¼-inch x fabric width strips for handles. Cut each strip into 30½-inch length.

- Cut one 4½ x 12½-inch strip for bag bottom.

From red print:
- Cut one 1½-inch x fabric width strip for flange.

- Cut two 6½-inch x fabric width strips. Subcut strips into two 6½ x 12½-inch rectangles, two 4½ x 6½-inch rectangles and one 4½ x 12½-inch rectangle for lining sides, ends and bottom.

- Cut one 1 x 12-inch strip for bag closures.

From black print:
- Cut two 2½ inch x fabric width strips for patchwork.

From thin cotton batting:
- Cut one 14 x 34-inch rectangle for bag body.

- Cut two 2¼ x 30½-inch strips for handles.

Assembly
Sew right sides together using ¼-inch seam allowances unless otherwise indicated.

Quilting Bag Body
1. Sew a 2½-inch x fabric width black/cream polka dot strip and a black print strip together along length; press seam toward polka dot strip. Repeat to make two strip sets.

2. Cut the strip sets into (24) 2½-inch units, referring to Figure 1.

Figure 1

3. Join the 2½-inch units into one 8-unit A row, two 2-unit B rows and two 6-unit C rows, referring to Figure 2.

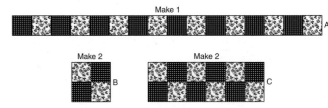

Figure 2

4. Sew B and C rows together beginning with B to make a B/C strip, referring to Figure 3. Stop stitching ¼ inch before end and backstitch (Figure 4); unsewn parts of seams will be along bottom edge of bag. Press seams open.

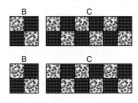

Figure 3

Figure 4

5. Spray-baste the A row and B/C strip and the black/cream polka dot bag bottom to the 14 x 34-inch cotton batting rectangle.

6. Quilt using the cream thread in an overall meandering pattern. Trim the batting close to the fabric. Set aside.

Constructing Bag Body

1. Fold and press the red print 1½-inch x fabric width strip in half lengthwise, wrong sides together.

2. Pin and sew the red print strip between the A row and B/C strip, matching raw edges and seams. Press seam toward B/C strip. Trim red strip even with edges (Figure 5).

Figure 5

3. Sew bag body together along 6½-inch side; stop stitching ¼ inch before bottom edge and backstitch, again referring to Figure 4. Press seam open.

4. Sew bag body to bag bottom matching bottom corners to body seams (Figure 6). Turn right side out.

Figure 6

Bag Lining

1. Sew together a red print 6½ x 12½-inch side rectangle and a red print 4½ x 6½-inch end rectangle along the 6½-inch edge. Begin stitching at lining top edge and stop ¼ inch from bottom edge of lining (refer to Figure 7). Backstitch at beginning and end of seam to secure. Repeat for second side/end unit.

Figure 7

2. Sew lining side/end units together to make lining body, referring to Figure 8. Press seams open.

Figure 8

3. Referring to Figure 8, pin and stitch lining body to lining bottom, matching lining bottom corners to lining body seams. *Do not turn right side out.*

Handles

1. Layer two 2¼ x 30½-inch black/cream polka dot strips, right sides together, with 2¼ x 30½-inch batting strip on top. Pin.

2. Use handle end template to trim both ends of each handle set (Figure 9).

Figure 9

3. Sew around all sides leaving a 3-inch opening on one side for turning. Clip curved handle ends and trim batting close to stitching.

4. Turn right side out. Press edges flat, turning opening edges to inside. Hand-stitch opening closed.

5. Repeat steps 1–4 for second handle. Topstitch around all edges of handles. Set aside.

Tie Closures

1. Press 1 x 12-inch red print strip lengthwise with edges to center. Fold and press 1-inch edges to wrong side, and then press strip in half lengthwise. Edgestitch together along lengthwise folded edges (Figure 10).

Figure 10

2. Cut strip in half. Tie a knot on finished end of each half.

3. Pin unknotted ends to center of right side of lining sides (Figure 11).

Figure 11

Completing Bag

1. Slip bag body into lining matching top raw edges and end seams. Pin and stitch around bag top leaving a 3-inch opening for turning. Turn right side out through opening.

2. Push lining into bag body and press bag top seam flat. Edgestitch around bag top keeping red ties free of stitching.

3. Fold top of end panel seams to center top of end panel and pin. Bar-tack folds together ½ inch from bag top edge by hand or machine (Figure 12). Repeat on opposite end.

Figure 12

4. Sew one ⅝-inch black button on each end over bar-tack.

5. Position and pin handles to sides, 3 inches from end seams and 3½ inches from top edge, referring to Figure 13. Sew handle ends through all layers, stitching over topstitching.

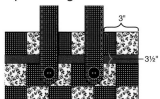

Figure 13

6. Center and sew 1-inch black buttons on ends of handles, again refering to Figure 13. ❖

Bag Handle
End Template

Sweet & Sassy

Use fun and fresh prints to create this small purse complete with prairie-point pocket accents and button embellishments.

Finished Size
10 x 10 x 3 inches

Materials
- 44/45-inch-wide 100-percent cotton fabrics:
    ⅔ yard dark red print
    ⅝ yard light yellow print
    ⅜ yard large floral print
- ¾ yard (44/45-inch-wide) thin cotton batting
- 3 (1-inch) dark red buttons
- 2 (¾-inch) dark red buttons
- 2 (½-inch) dark red buttons
- 6 inches ¾-inch-wide elastic
- 1 (1-inch) square hook-and-loop tape
- Coordinating quilting thread
- Basting adhesive spray
- Basic sewing supplies and equipment

Cutting

From dark red print:
- Cut one 2½-inch x fabric width strip. Subcut strip into four 2½-inch squares for prairie points and two 2½ x 6½-inch rectangles for pocket binding.
- Cut one 6-inch x fabric width strip for handle.
- Cut one 12 x 32-inch rectangle for purse body.

From light yellow print:
- Cut one 10½-inch x fabric width strip. Subcut into two 10½-inch squares for front and back lining, and three 3½ x 10½-inch rectangles for lining sides and bottom.
- Cut two 8 x 12-inch rectangles for pockets.
- Cut two 1½ x 6½-inch strips for casings.

From large floral print:
- Cut one 9-inch x fabric width strip. Subcut strip into one 9 x 20-inch rectangle, two 6½-inch squares for flap and six 2½-inch squares for prairie points.

From thin cotton batting:
- Cut one 12 x 32-inch rectangle.
- Cut one 9 x 20-inch rectangle.
- Cut one 8 x 12-inch rectangle.
- Cut one 6½-inch square.
- Cut one 2-inch x fabric width strip.

Quilting & Cutting Bag Body
1. Spray-baste the 12 x 32-inch batting rectangle to wrong side of same size dark red print fabric. Repeat with 9 x 20-inch rectangles of large floral print and batting.

2. Spray-baste the 8 x 12-inch batting rectangle between the 8 x 12-inch light yellow print rectangles, wrong sides to batting.

3. Quilt pieces with coordinating thread. Sample features an overall meandering pattern (Figure 1).

Figure 1

4. From the quilted dark red print 12 x 32-inch rectangle, cut three 3½ x 10½-inch rectangles for purse sides and bottom. Cut four 2½ x 10½-inch rectangles and two 2½ x 6½-inch rectangles for purse center-panel side/bottom borders.

5. From the quilted large floral print 9 x 20-inch rectangle, cut two 6½ x 8½-inch rectangles for purse front and back center panels.

6. From quilted light yellow print 8 x 12-inch rectangle, cut two 4½ x 6½-inch pockets.

Assembly

Sew right sides together using ¼-inch seam allowances unless otherwise indicated.

Purse Pockets

1. Press six large floral print and four dark red print 2½-inch squares in half diagonally, wrong sides together (Figure 2).

Figure 2

2. With folded edge at bottom, press triangle in half vertically (Figure 3), making prairie points.

Figure 3

3. Refer to Figure 4 to arrange three large floral print and two dark red print prairie points alternately on 6½-inch side of both 6½ x 4½-inch light yellow print quilted pockets matching raw edges and overlapping. Baste ⅛ inch from edge.

Figure 4

4. Press the 2½ x 6½-inch dark red print binding strips in half lengthwise, wrong sides together.

5. Pin and sew one strip over prairie points using a ½-inch seam and matching 6½-inch edges (Figure 5).

Figure 5

6. Press strip to opposite side of pocket, covering stitching and pin. Hand- or machine- stitch in place to bind pocket edge.

7. Repeat steps 5 and 6 on second pocket.

8. Pin pockets to bottom and sides of 6½ x 8½-inch large floral quilted center panels. Baste sides and bottom edges of pockets ⅛ inch from edges (Figure 6).

Figure 6

Constructing Purse Body

1. Sew dark red print 2½ x 6½-inch quilted bottom borders to center panel. Then sew 2½ x 10½-inch quilted side borders to center panel, referring to Figure 7. Press seams toward borders. Repeat with second center panel to make front and back of purse.

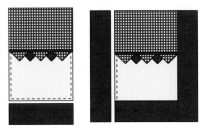

Figure 7

2. Sew a 3½ x 10½-inch dark red print quilted purse side rectangle to both 10½-inch sides of purse front. Stop stitching ¼ inch from bottom and back-stitch (Figure 8).

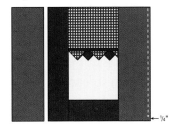

Figure 8

3. Sew purse back to the sides as in step 2, referring to Figure 9, completing purse body. Press seams open.

Figure 9   **Figure 10**

4. Sew purse body to 3½ x 10½-inch dark red print quilted bottom rectangle, matching corners to seams and pivoting at corners (Figure 10). Turn right side out.

5. To make purse flap, layer two 6½-inch large floral print squares, right sides together, on a 6½-inch thin cotton batting square.

6. Mark 1-inch from corner on top and sides of flap. Draw a diagonal line connecting marks. Trim triangle from corners (Figure 11).

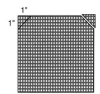

Figure 11

7. Sew fabric and batting squares together around sides and top, leaving edge opposite trimmed corners open. Trim batting close to stitching.

8. Turn right side out. Push out corners and press. Topstitch around flap edges. Quilt with coordinating thread and overall meandering pattern.

9. Position flap, right sides together, over the back center panel and baste ⅛ inch from edge (Figure 12).

Figure 12

Purse Handles

1. Press one long edge of 6-inch x fabric width dark red print strip ¼ inch to the wrong side. Center 2-inch x fabric width batting strip on wrong side of fabric strip.

2. Fold long raw edge of dark red print strip to center over batting and press. Fold long pressed edge over raw edge; press and pin (Figure 13).

Figure 13

3. Edgestitch center folded edge. Topstitch along sides (Figure 14).

Figure 14

4. Trim handle strip to desired handle length plus 9 inches. ***Note:*** *Sample handle strip was trimmed to 38 inches long to make a 29-inch handle.*

5. Press ends ¼ inch to wrong side.

6. Pin handle ends 4½ inches down from top edge and centered on purse sides, referring to Figure 15.

Figure 15

7. Double edgestitch across handle end. Beginning ½ inch from top edge, stitch handle to purse along handle topstitching.

8. Pull handle down away from top edge and pin to hold away from top.

Purse Lining

1. Sew two 3½ x 10½-inch light yellow print lining sides and two 10½-inch-square light yellow print linings (front and back) together on the 10½-inch edges. Refer to steps 2 and 3 and Figures 8 and 9 of Constructing Purse Body.

2. Sew 3½ x 10½-inch light yellow print lining bottom to lining body referring to step 4 and Figure 10 of Constructing Purse Body. *Do not turn right side out.*

3. Press ends and sides of 1½ x 6½-inch light yellow print strips ¼ inch to the wrong side to form casings.

4. Pin casings ¾ inch from top of lining, centered over lining side panels, referring to Figure 16. Edgestitch long sides of casing, leaving ends open.

Figure 16

Completing Purse

1. Slip purse body into lining, right sides together. Match raw edges and seams and keep handles away from top edge. Sew around top edge leaving opening at flap area for turning.

2. Turn right side out. Push lining into purse body. Press top edge flat turning opening edge to inside. Hand-stitch opening closed or edgestitch around top edge.

3. Pull handle ends up and pin at top edge. Edgestitch around top keeping flap pulled up from seam but securing handle (Figure 17).

Figure 17

4. Sew 1-inch button centered and ½ inch up from handle end. Sew one each ¾-inch button and ½-inch button ½ inch apart, referring to Figure 18. Repeat on opposite handle end.

Figure 18

5. Cut 6-inch ¾-inch elastic piece in half. Insert 3-inch piece of elastic into casing with safety pin or bodkin. Slowly pull elastic through casing until elastic end is even with casing end. Pin and double edgestitch through all layers across casing end making sure to catch the elastic.

6. Pull elastic through casing, securing opposite end as in step 5.

7. Sew hook side of 1-inch square hook-and-loop tape centered on center panel and 1-inch above pocket (Figure 19).

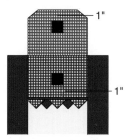

Figure 19

8. Sew loop side of hook-and-loop tape square centered on wrong side of flap and 1 inch from edge.

9. Sew 1-inch button on right side of flap over hook-and-loop tape square. ❖

Batik Butterfly Shopping Tote

Choose different fabrics to change the capabilities of this lightweight tote. Outdoor canvas for the tote body and belting for the handles will create a shopping bag with the strength to handle a quick trip to the grocery store with ease. Home decor fabrics lend a carpet-bag look for an on-the-go sewing or needlework project tote.

Finished Size
19 x 14 x 5 inches

Materials
- 44/45-inch-wide 100-percent cotton fabrics:
  1½ yards black batik print
  ¼ yard pink batik
- 4½ x 14-inch rectangle heavy cardboard
- Coordinating all-purpose thread
- Basic sewing supplies and equipment

Cutting

From black batik print:
- Cut one 20½-inch x fabric width rectangle for tote body.

- Cut two 8½ x 12½-inch rectangles for pockets.

- Cut one 5½ x 29-inch rectangle for bottom cardboard cover.

- Cut two 5½-inch x fabric width strips for handles.

From pink batik:
- Cut one 4½-inch x fabric width strip. Subcut two 4½ x 20½-inch strips for tote top band.

- Cut one 1½-inch x fabric width strip. Subcut two 1½ x 8½-inch strips for pocket bands.

Assembly
Sew right sides together using ¼-inch seam allowances unless otherwise indicated.

Tote Pockets
1. Fold and press pink batik 1½ x 8½-inch pocket band in half lengthwise wrong sides together.

2. Match raw edges and pin pocket band to right side of one 8½-inch end of an 8½ x 12½-inch black batik print pocket (Figure 1). Baste band in place using a ⅛" seam allowance.

Figure 1

3. Fold pocket with right sides together matching all edges. Stitch around sides and top leaving a 3-inch opening for turning on one side (Figure 2).

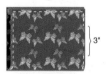

Figure 2

4. Trim corners close to stitching (Figure 3). Turn pocket right side out and use a point turner to push corners out. Turn opening seam allowances to inside and press pocket flat.

Figure 3

5. Repeat steps 1–4 to make second pocket. Set pockets aside.

Tote Handle

1. Fold and press two 5½-inch x fabric width black batik print strips, right sides together, in half length-wise. Stitch together both ends and along length leaving a 3-inch opening for turning (Figure 4).

Figure 4

2. Trim corners close to stitching, referring to Figure 3. Turn right side out and use a point turner to turn corners. Turn opening seam allowances to inside and press flat.

3. Edgestitch ⅛-inch from all edges. Set handles aside.

Tote Bottom

1. Press ¼-inch to wrong side on both 5½-inch ends of the 5½ x 29-inch black batik print bottom card-board cover rectangle (Figure 5).

Figure 5

2. Press ¼-inch to wrong side again on both ends to make a ¼-inch double-turned hem. Edgestitch along first fold (Figure 6).

Figure 6

3. Fold bottom cardboard cover in half with right sides together matching hemmed ends and raw sides. Sew side seams and finish seams with a zigzag or overcast stitch.

4. Turn right side out. Insert 4½ x 14-inch heavy-weight cardboard rectangle and set aside. *Note: You can substitute a piece of plastic, like kitchen plastic cutting mats, cut to size.*

Completing Tote

1. Fold both 4½ x 20½-inch pink batik top band strips in half lengthwise with wrong sides together and press.

2. Pin one band on wrong side of 20½-inch x fabric width black batik print tote body rectangle along the 20½-inch edge matching raw edges and stitch (Figure 7). Press top band to right side.

Figure 7

3. Repeat with second top band on opposite end of tote body.

4. Fold the tote body in half lengthwise and press. Unfold and measure 7 inches from each end of tote body along center fold and mark with a pin for pocket positions (Figure 8).

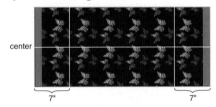

Figure 8

5. Mark center of pocket tops and bottoms with a pin. Position one pocket with top at 7-inch mark on one end of tote body matching pocket centers with center crease of tote body.

6. Pin and edgestitch ⅛ inch from pocket sides and bottom through all thicknesses (Figure 9).

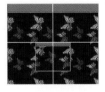

Figure 9

Note: To make a more secure pocket top edge, stitch a triangle on the top corners rather than just back-stitching to secure the corners (Figure 10).

Figure 10

7. Repeat with second pocket on opposite end.

8. Position one handle end on either side of a pocket with ends even with bottom of pocket. Pin in place.

9. Sew in place stitching over handle edgestitching and across bottom of tote top band through all thicknesses (Figure 11).

Figure 11

10. Repeat with second handle on opposite side of tote.

11. Fold the tote body with right sides together matching the top band and sides. Pin in place (Figure 12).

Figure 12

12. Sew side seams, backstitching several times at top of tote to secure. Finish seams with zigzag or overcast stitch.

13. Lightly press across bottom of tote to mark center.

14. To make box bottom, match side seams to bottom center crease. Mark seam line 2½ inches from corner, perpendicular to side seam and sew (Figure 13).

Figure 13

15. Trim seam to ¼ inch and finish seam with a zigzag or overcast stitch.

16. Turn tote right side out and insert cardboard bottom. ❖

Batik Butterfly Mini Purse

Here's the perfect mini purse to store all your essentials from business cards to photos to your little stash of cash. No need to carry a heavy purse. Simply wear it like a necklace, and you're ready to go with everything you need at your fingertips.

Finished Size
5 x 6½ inches

Materials
- 44/45-inch-wide 100-percent cotton fabrics:
  ½ yard black batik print
  ⅛ yard pink batik
- Coordinating all-purpose thread
- Basic sewing supplies and equipment

Cutting

From black batik print:
- Cut two 5½-inch x fabric width strips. Subcut four 5½ x 6½-inch rectangles for body and lining; four 5½ x 5½-inch squares for pockets A and four 3½ x 5½-inch rectangles for pockets B.

- Cut one 1½-inch x fabric width strip for shoulder strap.

From pink batik:
- Cut one 1½-inch x fabric width strip. Subcut one 1½ x 10½-inch strip, for purse top band and one 1 x 24-inch strip for pocket trims.

Assembly
Sew right sides together using ¼-inch seam allowances unless otherwise indicated.

1. Fold and press 1 x 24-inch pink batik pocket trim strip, wrong sides together, in half lengthwise.

2. Cut into four 5½-inch lengths.

3. Match raw edges and pin pink batik trim pieces to right sides of two pocket A squares and two pocket B rectangles along 5½-inch sides. Baste ⅛-inch from raw edges (Figure 1).

Figure 1

4. Pin a pocket A square, right sides together, along the trim top edge of a pocket A square from step 3. Sew edges together (Figure 2).

Figure 2

5. Turn right side out with trim at top; press. Baste sides and bottom ⅛-inch from edges (Figure 3).

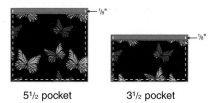

5½ pocket   3½ pocket

Figure 3

6. Repeat steps 4 and 5 with remaining pocket A squares and B rectangles to make two A pockets and two B pockets.

7. Cut 1½ x 10½-inch pink batik top band strip into two 5½-inch lengths.

8. Press ¼-inch to wrong side on one long edge of both band strips.

9. Matching raw edges, baste a pink batik band along one 5½-inch edge of two 5½ x 6½-inch black batik print rectangles for purse body.

10. Press pink batik band along seam line away from black batik print (Figure 4).

Figure 4

11. Matching side and bottom raw edges, layer an A pocket, then a B pocket on the right side of a purse body rectangle. Baste together ⅛ inch from sides and bottom edges (Figure 5).

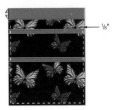

Figure 5

12. Repeat with remaining purse body rectangle and pockets to make second side of purse.

13. Sew purse sides, right sides together, matching pockets, side edges and bottom.

14. Trim corners close to stitching. Turn right side out using a point turner to turn corners. Fold pink batik band down (Figure 6).

Figure 6

15. Sew remaining two 5½ x 6½-inch rectangles together along sides and bottom for lining. *Do not turn right side out.*

16. Insert lining into purse.

17. Match side seams and top raw edge. Pin and sew around top of purse (Figure 7).

Figure 7

18. Fold pink batik band to purse lining side, covering top seam and hand-stitch in place (Figure 8).

Figure 8

Purse Strap

1. Press long raw edges of 1½-inch x fabric width strip black batik print shoulder strap to center of strip (Figure 9a). Then press strip in half lengthwise (Figure 9b).

Figure 9

2. Edgestitch shoulder strap together along long edges. Finish one raw end with zigzag or overcast stitch.

3. Trim unfinished end to adjust strap length. Sample is 36 inches plus 2 inches for attaching to purse for a total of 38 inches. Finish trimmed end with zigzag or overcast stitch.

4. Hand-stitch strap to purse, stitching 1-inch of each end of strap to lining side seams (Figure 10).

Figure 10

Note: For a stronger strap application, turn strap ends under ¼ inch and center the strap ends ¾ inch from the top, over side seams on right side of purse. Machine stitch through all thicknesses across the purse top and over original stitching on strap sides and bottom. Or use a machine specialty stitch to attach strap ends to purse. ❖

Posy Patchwork

Romantic florals and soft colors add style to any purse for day or evening. Ruched flower accents provide the perfect finishing touch.

Finished Size
10 x 10 x 4 inches

Materials
- 44/45-inch-wide 100-percent cotton fabrics:
    - ⅝ yard light green print
    - ½ yard pink print
    - ½ yard light blue floral print
    - ½ yard blue floral stripe
- ⅞ yard thin cotton batting
- Cream thread for quilting
- Basting adhesive spray
- Basic sewing supplies and equipment

Cutting

From light green print:
- Cut one 12½-inch x fabric width strip for bag body.

- Cut one 4½-inch x fabric width strip. Subcut into two 4½ x 10½-inch rectangles for bag side pockets and two 4½ x 4½-inch squares for bag end pockets.

From pink print:
- Cut one 4½-inch x fabric width strip. Subcut into seven 2½ x 4½-inch rectangles for pocket patchwork strip.

- Cut one 2½-inch x fabric width strip for binding.

- Cut one 5½-inch x fabric width strip. Trim to 34 inches long for handle.

From light blue floral print:
- Cut one 4½-inch x fabric width strip. Subcut into seven 2½ x 4½-inch rectangles for pocket patchwork strip.

- Cut one 8½-inch x fabric width strip. Subcut into two 8½ x 10½-inch rectangles for side pocket linings and two 4½ x 8½-inch rectangles for end pocket linings.

From blue floral stripe:
- Cut one 10½-inch x fabric width strip. Subcut into two 10½ x 10½-inch squares for lining sides and three 4½ x 10½-inch rectangles for lining ends and bottom.

- Cut one 2½-inch x fabric width strip for ruched flowers.

From thin cotton batting:
- Cut one 12½ x 40-inch rectangle for bag body.

- Cut one 10½ x 40-inch rectangle for bag pockets.

- Cut one 2½ x 34-inch strip for handle.

Assembly

Sew right sides together using ¼-inch seam allowances unless otherwise indicated.

Quilting Bag Body

1. Spray-baste the 12½ x 40-inch cotton batting rectangle to the wrong side of the 12½-inch x fabric width light green print rectangle.

2. Quilt batting and light green print together using the cream thread in an overall meandering pattern referring to Figure 1.

Figure 1

3. Cut the quilted piece into two 10½ x 10½-inch bag side rectangles, two 4½ x 10½-inch bag end rectangles, and one 4½ x 10½-inch bag bottom rectangle. Set pieces aside for use in Constructing Bag Body.

Bag Pockets

1. Sew light blue floral print and light pink 2½ x 4½-inch rectangles together along the 4½-inch edges making two sets of five rectangles (A, C) and two sets of two rectangles (B, D). Refer to Figure 2 for color arrangements. Press seams toward light blue floral.

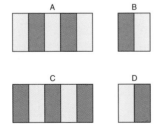

Figure 2

2. Sew set A to a 4½ x 10½-inch light green bag side pocket (Figure 3). Press seam toward light green piece. Repeat with set C making two side pockets.

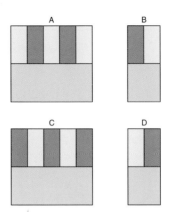

Figure 3

3. Sew set B to a 4½ x 4½-inch light green print bag end pocket, again referring to Figure 3. Press seam toward light green piece. Repeat with set D making two end pockets.

4. Layer and spray-baste the two end pockets and the two side pockets onto the 10½ x 40-inch thin cotton batting as in step 1 of Quilting Bag Body. Quilt together using the cream thread, referring to step 2 of Quilting Bag Body and Figure 1.

5. Trim batting even with pocket pieces. Sew quilted pockets right sides together with same size pocket linings along the pieced edges. Press linings to wrong side of pocket. Baste linings and pockets together along raw edges.

Constructing Bag Body

1. Pin side pocket A to a light green quilted 10½-inch square side matching side and bottom edges (Figure 4). Baste together ⅛ inch from raw edges to make side A unit.

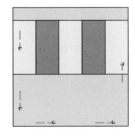

Figure 4

2. Repeat to make side C unit and two end units B and D, using quilted 4½ x 10½-inch bag ends with end pockets.

3. Match vertical edge of bag side A unit and 10½-inch edge of bag end B unit referring to Figure 5. Sew units together beginning at bag top and stopping ¼ inch from bag bottom, again referring to Figure 5. Backstitch at beginning and end of seam to secure. Repeat with side C unit and end D unit.

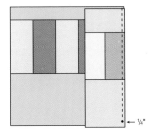

Figure 5

4. Sew bag side and end units together. Refer to Figure 6 and step 3 to make bag body. Press seams open.

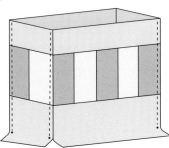

Figure 6

5. Pin and stitch bag body to quilted bag bottom matching bottom corners to body seams (Figure 7). Turn right side out.

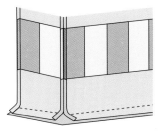

Figure 7

Completing Bag

1. Sew blue floral stripe lining pieces together following steps 3 through 5 of Constructing Bag Body. *Do not turn right side out.*

2. Slip lining inside the bag body, wrong sides together, matching raw edges and seams.

3. Fold and press 2½-inch x fabric width pink binding strip in half lengthwise, wrong sides together.

4. Measure top edge of bag and add ½ inch. Trim strip to this length.

5. Open out strip and sew short ends with right sides together. Press seam flat. Refold strip and press.

6. Pin and sew strip to right side of bag top matching raw edges (Figure 8). Press strip to lining side. Hand-stitch binding in place over raw edges and stitching line.

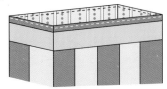

Figure 8

7. Along one long edge of the 5½ x 34-inch pink print handle strip, press ¼ inch to the wrong side. Press opposite edge 1½ inches to wrong side. Fold pressed edge 1¼ inch to wrong side overlapping opposite raw edge and press (Figure 9).

Figure 9

8. Open handle strip. Position and spray-baste the 2½ x 34-inch cotton batting strip in the center of the handle strip. Refold first raw edge and then pressed edge of handle strip over batting and pin along pressed edge to hold. *This is the wrong side of the handle.*

9. Edgestitch along the pinned pressed edge. Topstitch along both outside edges. Press short ends up ½ inch toward the right side of fabric (Figure 10).

Figure 10

10. Center ends of handles on bag ends, right sides together with lining, 1 inch from bag top and pin (Figure 11).

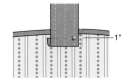

Figure 11

11. Edgestitch along folded handle end. Sew two more lines of stitching parallel to first row, ¼ and ½ inch from bag top edge (Figure 12).

Figure 12

Making the Ruched Flowers

1. Cut the 2½-inch x fabric width blue floral stripe strip in half. Press the short ends ½ inch to wrong side.

2. Fold both pieces in half lengthwise, right sides together, and sew along long raw edges. Turn pieces right side out. Press seam only flat.

3. Hand-stitch large gathering stitches in a zigzag along the seam of both pieces with a double thread (Figure 13). Pull gathering stitches until the strips measure 8 inches long.

Figure 13

4. Gently roll the ruched fabric strip into a flower shape. Tack edges at bottom layer of flower to hold flower shape.

5. Hand-stitch the flowers to each end of the bag over handle stitching (Figure 14). ❖

Figure 14

Ragtime Blues

Enjoy the fun and fuzzy technique of rag seams to make this cute and functional bag—complete with a removable organizer (see page 34) that lets you transfer in minutes all of your necessities. It's a real timesaver!

Finished Size
7 x 12 x 4 inches

Materials
- 44/45-inch-wide 100-percent cotton fabrics:
  ⅔ yard medium blue print
  ⅝ yard light blue mottled
  ½ yard dark blue mottled
- ⅜ yard (44/45-inch-wide) thin cotton batting
- 1 yard ¼-inch cotton cord
- 1 (1-inch) dark blue button
- 1 (⅜-inch) medium blue button
- Coordinating quilting thread
- Basting adhesive spray
- Basic sewing supplies and equipment

Cutting

From medium blue print:
- Cut three 5-inch x fabric width strips. Subcut 12 (5-inch) squares for body and two 5 x 13-inch rectangles for bottom.
- Cut two 2½-inch x fabric width strips for handles.
- Cut eight 2 x 2½-inch rectangles for handle tabs.
- Cut one 1½ x 9-inch strip for button loop.

From light blue mottled:
- Cut two 5-inch x fabric width strips. Subcut 12 (5-inch) squares for body.
- Cut two 2½-inch x fabric width strips for handles.

From dark blue mottled:
- Cut eight 5-inch squares for body.
- Cut two 2½-inch x fabric width strips for handles.

From thin cotton batting:
- Cut 16 (4-inch) squares.
- Cut one 4 x 12-inch rectangle.

Assembly
Sew right sides together using ½-inch seam allowances unless otherwise indicated.

Quilting Bag Body
1. Sort 5-inch squares into same fabric pairs, wrong sides together: six pairs each of medium blue print and light blue mottled, and four pairs of dark blue mottled.

2. Spray-baste a 4-inch thin cotton batting square centered between each pair of squares.

3. Repeat step 2 with the two medium blue print 5 x 13-inch rectangles, wrong sides together, and the 4 x 12-inch thin cotton batting rectangle.

4. Quilt rectangle and all 16 square pairs with an allover meandering pattern. *Do not quilt in the ½-inch seam allowance* (Figure 1).

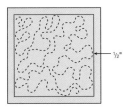

Figure 1

Constructing Bag Body
Note: *In order to achieve the "raggedy" look, seam allowances will be kept on the right side of the bag. Sew all seams ½-inch wide unless otherwise indicated.*

1. Sew quilted squares together into 13 x 9-inch front and back units and 5 x 9-inch end units. Refer to Figure 2 for color placement.

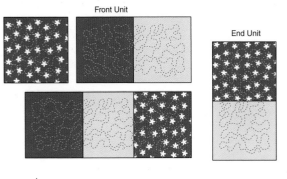

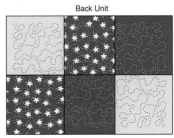

Figure 2

2. With wrong sides together, sew front and back units to end units on the 9-inch sides; stop stitching and backstitch ¼ inch from bottom end of each seam to make bag body (Figure 3). *Note: Mark your bottom ends with washable pencil so you don't reverse the pieces when sewing to the bag bottom.*

Figure 3

3. With wrong sides together, sew the bag body to the quilted 5 x 13-inch bag bottom, matching side seams to corners and pivoting at corners (Figure 4).

Figure 4

4. Referring to the side with seam allowances as right side of bag, fold top edge of purse to right side 1½ inches. Measure 1-inch below top fold and sew around the purse to form a casing, leaving a 2-inch opening at back of purse (Figure 5).

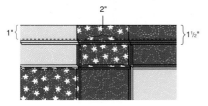

Figure 5

5. Using a safety pin or bodkin, thread the ¼-inch cotton cord through the casing. Sew cord ends together and insert in casing. Hand- or machine-stitch opening closed.

6. Clip all seam allowances ¼ inch apart close to the stitching line. Cut carefully so you don't cut through the stitching line (Figure 6). Wash and dry bag to ravel seam allowances. Remove lint and extra threads.

Figure 6

Handles & Tabs

1. Fold a light blue mottled 2½-inch x fabric width strip in half lengthwise, right sides together. Stitch length together and turn right side out. Repeat to make two tubes each of light blue mottled, dark blue mottled and medium blue print.

2. Match short ends of one of each color strip and double-stitch together ¼ inch from end (Figure 7). Braid strips together, pinning ends together when completed. Repeat to make two handles.

Figure 7

3. Measure from sewn end and mark handle length desired with a pin. Double-stitch across braid to secure. Trim to ¼-inch seam allowance. Repeat on second handle.

4. Center handle ends 1½ inches below top edge on the outside two squares of bag front and double-stitch through all thicknesses (Figure 8). Repeat to place handles on back of bag.

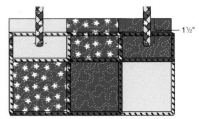

Figure 8

5. Using a ¼-inch seam, sew two 2 x 2½-inch medium blue print rectangles handle tabs together around all sides, leaving a 1-inch opening for turning on one side. Trim corners and turn right side out. Press and turn opening seam to inside. Repeat to make four handle tabs.

6. Position tabs over handle ends and edgestitch around tabs through all thicknesses (Figure 9).

Figure 9

Button Loop & Button

1. Press long edges of 1½ x 9-inch medium blue print strip to center. Press in half, folded edges together. Edgestitch folded long edges together.

2. Fold strip in half, matching raw ends to create button loop. Position loop at center back of bag, raw ends even with casing seam allowance. Sew loop in place over casing seam referring to Figure 10.

Figure 10

3. Place the ⅜-inch medium blue button on top of the 1-inch dark blue button. Center the buttons on front center square of bag approximately 1 inch below casing seam. Hand-stitch buttons to attach to bag (Figure 11). ❖

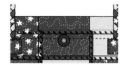

Figure 11

Switchable Organizer

This handy organizer easily slips into a new purse for a quick-change fashion makeover. The pockets keep everything organized and at your fingertips.

Finished Size
10 x 10 x 4 inches

Materials
- 44/45-inch-wide 100-percent cotton fabrics:
  - ⅓ yard light blue mottled
  - ⅓ yard dark blue mottled
  - ¼ yard medium blue print
- ⅓ yard (22-inch-wide) mediumweight interfacing
- ⅛ yard (22-inch-wide) heavyweight interfacing
- Basic sewing supplies and equipment

Cutting

From light blue mottled for organizer:
- Cut one 10½-inch x fabric width strip. Subcut two 6½ x 10½-inch rectangles for front and back, two 4½ x 6½-inch rectangles for ends, one 4½ x 10½-inch rectangle for bottom and two 1½ x 6½-inch strips for handles.

From dark blue mottled for lining:
- Cut one 6½-inch x fabric width strip. Subcut two 6½ x 10½-inch rectangles for lining front and back, and two 4½ x 6½-inch rectangles for lining ends.

From medium blue print for lining pockets:
- Cut two 5½-inch x fabric width strips. Subcut into four 5½ x 10½-inch rectangles for front and back pockets, four 4½ x 6½ inch-rectangles for end pockets and one 4½ x 10½-inch rectangle for lining bottom.

From mediumweight interfacing:
- Cut two 6½ x 10½-inch rectangles.
- Cut two 4½ x 6½-inch rectangles.

From heavyweight interfacing:
- Cut one 4½ x 10½-inch rectangle.

Assembly
Sew right sides together using ½-inch seam allowances unless otherwise indicated.

1. With right sides together, sew two medium blue print 5½ x 10½-inch rectangles together along one 10½-inch side. Turn right side out. Press and edgestitch, referring to Figure 1. Repeat to make front and back pockets.

Figure 1

2. With right sides together, sew two medium blue print 4½ x 6½-inch rectangles together along one 4½-inch side. Turn right side out. Press and edgestich, referring to Figure 1. Repeat to make two end pockets.

3. Referring to Figure 2, mark stitching lines for pocket sections as desired. You may want pocket areas for cell phone, pens, lipstick, checkbook, etc.

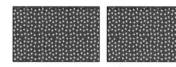

Figure 2

4. Place all mediumweight interfacing rectangles on wrong sides of all same size dark blue mottled rectangles and baste ⅛ inch from edges.

5. Layer and pin pocket sections on right side of dark blue mottled rectangles matching side and bottom edges (Figure 3). Sew together ⅛ inch from edges.

Figure 3

6. Sew through all layers on marked pocket section lines.

7. Sew the constructed lining pocket front, back and sides together alternately on 6½-inch sides; stop stitching and backstitch ¼ inch from bottom edge (Figure 4). Press seams open.

Figure 4

8. Baste heavyweight interfacing to wrong side of medium blue print 4½ x 10½-inch bottom rectangle. Trim interfacing close to stitching.

9. Pin and stitch lining body to bottom, matching bottom corners to lining seams and pivoting at corners (Figure 5). *Do not turn right side out.*

Figure 5

10. Sew light blue mottled 6½ x 10½-inch front and back rectangles and 4½ x 6½-inch end rectangles together alternately on 6½-inch sides. Stop stitching and backstitch ¼ inch from bottom to make organizer body (refer to Figure 4). Press seams open.

11. Pin organizer body to light blue mottled 4½ x 10½-inch bottom, matching bottom corners to seams. Stitch seams, pivoting at corners (refer to Figure 5). Turn right side out.

12. Press long edges of both 1½ x 6½-inch light blue mottled strips to center. Then press in half lengthwise. Edgestitch folded edges together (Figure 6).

Figure 6

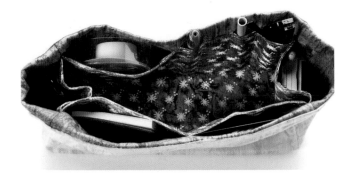

13. Fold strips in half to create loops. Pin one loop to each end of organizer, raw ends of loops to the right side of organizer (Figure 7). Baste in place.

Figure 7

14. Slip the organizer body into the lining, right sides together. Match top edges and seams and pin in place. Sew around the top leaving a 4-inch opening for turning.

15. Turn right side out, pushing lining into the organizer bag and pulling loops up. Press top seam flat, turning opening edges to inside. Hand-stitch opening closed or edgestitch top edge. ❖

Tip

For a sturdier bottom base, use lightweight plastic instead of heavyweight interfacing. Choices include: quilting template plastic, plastic canvas or kitchen cutting mat sheets. Do not sew the plastic to the lining bottom. Cut plastic the purse bottom size, without seam allowances, and insert into organizer after turning right side out and before stitching top edge closed.

Gathered Go-Go Purse

Fun and flirty, this cute medium-size purse is perfect for any occasion. Choose fabrics to match your ensemble or use neutral fabrics to create an everyday bag.

Finished Size
10 x 12 x 4 inches

Materials
- 44/45-inch-wide 100-percent cotton fabrics:
    - 1⅛ yards deep pink print
    - ¼ yard dark purple print
    - ¼ yard blue-gray print
- ¾ yard lightweight batting (or 1 package fusible craft fleece)
- Coordinating all-purpose thread
- Basic sewing supplies and equipment

Cutting

From deep pink print:
- Cut two 4½-inch x fabric width strips. Subcut strips into one each 4½ x 28½-inch strip for top band, 4½ x 14½-inch rectangle for lining bottom, 4½ x 10½-inch rectangle for purse bottom and 4½ x 3½-inch rectangle for bow knot; and two 4½ x 6½-inch rectangles for bow.

- Cut one 2½ x 28½-inch strip for center band.

- Cut one 10½-inch x fabric width strip. Subcut two 10½ x 14½-inch rectangles for lining body.

- Cut two 5 x 36-inch strips for purse handles.

From dark purple print:
- Cut one 4½-inch x fabric width strip for gathered band.

From blue-gray print:
- Cut one 4½-inch x fabric width strip for gathered band.

From lightweight batting:
- Cut two 2 x 36-inch strips.

- Cut one 2 x 28½-inch strip.

- Cut two 14½ x 10½-inch rectangles.

- Cut one 14½ x 4½-inch rectangle.

Assembly
Sew right sides together using a ¼-inch seam unless otherwise indicated.

Purse Lining
1. Baste 14½ x 10½-inch and 14½ x 4½-inch lightweight batting pieces to wrong side of same size deep pink lining pieces ⅛ inch from all sides.

2. Pin and sew a 14½ x 10½-inch lining rectangle to both 14½-inch sides of the 14½ x 4½-inch lining bottom, referring to Figure 1.

14½"

10½"

4½"

10½"

Figure 1

House of White Birches, Berne, Indiana 46711 Clotilde.com

3. Fold in half, matching seams and 14½-inch sides; press. Sew side seams together (Figure 2). Press seams open.

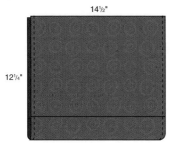

14½"

12¼"

Figure 2

4. To box bottom, match side seams to pressed fold in lining bottom pulling corners out into a point.

5. Sew 2 inches from corner points along bottom side seams (Figure 3).

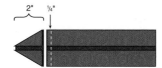

2"   ¼"

Figure 3

6. Trim seam allowances to ¼ inch, referring to Figure 3. *Do not turn right side out.* Set aside.

Purse Handles

1. Center 2 x 36-inch batting strip lengthwise on wrong side of 5 x 36-inch deep pink handle strip (Figure 4a). Press one raw edge of deep pink handle strip 1½ inches over batting to center (Figure 4b).

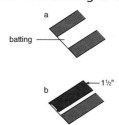

a

batting

b   1½"

Figure 4

2. Press opposite side of deep pink strip ½ inch to wrong side (Figure 5a). Then press strip edge 1 inch to center over raw edge (Figure 5b). Pin in place.

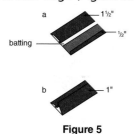

a   1½"

batting   ½"

b   1"

Figure 5

3. Edgestitch along center fold. Topstitch ¼-inch from each outside edge (Figure 6).

Figure 6

4. Adjust handle lengths by trimming to desired length plus 5 inches. For a 30-inch finished handle, trim handles to 35 inches.

5. Turn handle ends ½ inch to right side of handle. Press and pin to hold. Set aside.

Bow

1. With right sides facing, sew the two 4½ x 6½-inch deep pink rectangles together around all edges leaving a 2-inch opening for turning along one 6½-inch side.

2. Trim corners close to stitching (Figure 7) and turn right side out. Push corners out with a point turner.

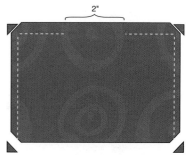

2"

Figure 7

3. Turn opening seam allowances to inside and hand-stitch closed. Press flat.

4. Fold deep pink 4½ x 3½-inch rectangle in half right sides together matching 4½-inch sides. Sew along one end and the 4½-inch side (Figure 8). Trim corners and turn right side out.

Figure 8

5. Wrap small rectangle around center of larger rectangle. Pull sewn end over raw edge snug to make a bow (Figure 9). Hand-stitch small rectangle end to itself to secure. Set aside.

Figure 9

Purse Body

1. Sew gathering stitches ⅛ inch and ⅜ inch from both long edges of the dark purple and blue-gray 4½-inch x fabric width strips for gathered bands (Figure 10).

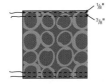

Figure 10

2. Gather strips to measure 28½ inches long. Secure gathering by placing a pin at seam lines and wrapping thread around pin referring to Figure 11.

Figure 11

3. Pin and sew dark purple gathered band to deep pink 2½ x 28½-inch center band. Adjust gathers on dark purple band to match if necessary. Remove gathering stitches. Press seam toward center band.

4. Repeat step 3 with blue-gray gathered strip on opposite long side of deep pink center band (Figure 12).

Figure 12

5. Fold purse body in half and sew side seams together, matching top and bottom raw edges. Stop stitching ¼-inch from bottom edge of blue-gray band and backstitch (Figure 13).

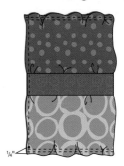

Figure 13

6. Position and pin blue-gray edge of purse seam at one corner of deep pink 4½ x 10½-inch purse bottom. Continue to pin blue-gray gathered band around purse bottom, adjusting gathers as needed. Sew gathered band to purse bottom, pivoting at corners (Figure 14). *Note: Reducing stitch length close to corners will make pivoting easier and add extra strength to corners.*

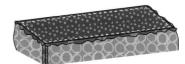

Figure 14

7. Clip blue-gray seam allowance almost to corner point (Figure 15). Remove gathering stitches. Press seam toward purse bottom. Turn purse body right side out.

Figure 15

Completing Purse

1. Insert lining into purse body, wrong sides together. Push lining into bottom corners and match top raw edges. Pin to secure top.

2. Fold and press 4½ x 28½-inch deep pink top band in half lengthwise with wrong sides together.

3. Unfold and position 2 x 28½-inch batting strip next to center crease. Baste to secure (Figure 16).

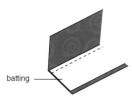

batting

Figure 16

4. Fold over and press ¼-inch of top band over batting edge (Figure 17).

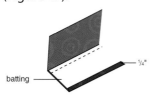

batting — ¼"

Figure 17

5. Open flat and sew short ends of top band together.

6. Matching side seams and raw edges, sew dark purple gathered band to raw edge of top band, adjusting gathers as necessary. Remove gathering stitches. Press seam toward top band. Turn purse inside out to lining side.

7. Fold top band over to lining side covering seam allowance. Hand-stitch in place.

8. Pin one handle end to lining side of top band touching the band side seam with right sides toward lining and with folded edge at top-band seam (Figure 18).

Figure 18

9. Edgestitch handle ends along sides and bottom and at band top. Stitch an X in stitched square referring to Figure 19.

Figure 19

10. Position the other end of handle, 6 inches from first. Refer to step 9 to secure in place.

11. Secure second handle's ends on other side of purse top opposite the first handle's ends, referring to step 9 and Figure 18 to secure. Turn purse right side out.

12. Hand-stitch bow to purse front at an angle over the center band referring to photo. ❖

On the Go

This bag is a little more challenging, but worth the effort. Embellished with a braided handle and decorative grommets, it easily accessorizes jeans and a T-shirt, or a perky workday ensemble.

Finished Size
8 x 10 x 4 inches

Materials
- 44/45-inch-wide 100-percent cotton fabrics:
    - 1⅛ yards orange print
    - 1 yard brown print
    - ⅞ yard cream print
- ⅔ yard cotton batting
- 4 (2-inch) plastic grommets
- Coordinating variegated thread for quilting
- Basting adhesive spray
- Basic sewing supplies and equipment

Cutting

From orange print:
- Cut one 12½-inch x fabric width strip for bag body.
- Cut one 10½-inch x fabric width strip. Subcut strip into two 8½ x 10½-inch rectangles for lining sides, two 4½ x 10½-inch rectangles for lining ends and one 4½ x 8½-inch rectangle for lining bottom.
- Cut two 5-inch x fabric width strips for braided handle and embellishment.

From brown print:
- Cut one 2½-inch x fabric width strip. Subcut strip into six 2½ x 4½-inch rectangles for triangle units.
- Cut one 4½-inch x fabric width strip. Subcut strip into two 4½ x 8½-inch rectangles for outside side pockets, and two 4½ x 4½-inch squares for outside end pockets.
- Cut two 6½-inch x fabric width strips. Subcut one strip into a 6½ x 24½-inch rectangle for bag top band. Subcut second strip into two 6½ x 8½-inch rectangles for outside side pocket linings, and two 4½ x 6½-inch rectangles for outside end pocket linings.
- Cut two 5-inch x fabric width strips for braided handle and embellishment.

From cream print:
- Cut two 6½-inch x fabric width strips. Subcut strips into four 6½ x 8½-inch rectangles and four 4½ x 6½-inch rectangles for lining pockets.
- Cut one 2½-inch x fabric width strip. Subcut strip into (12) 2½ x 2½-inch squares for triangle units.
- Cut two 5-inch x fabric width strips for braided handle and embellishment.

From cotton batting:
- Cut one 12½ x 36-inch piece for bag body.
- Cut two 6½ x 8½-inch rectangles for outside side pockets.
- Cut two 4½ x 6½-inch rectangles for outside end pockets.

Assembly
Sew right sides together using ¼-inch seam allowances unless otherwise indicated.

Quilting Bag Body
1. Spray-baste the 12½ x 36-inch cotton batting strip to the wrong side of the 12½-inch x fabric width orange print strip.

2. Quilt batting and orange print together using variegated thread in an overall meandering pattern, referring to Figure 1.

Figure 1

3. Cut the quilted piece into two 8½ x 10½-inch bag side rectangles, two 4½ x 10½-inch bag end rectangles and one 4½ x 8½-inch bag bottom rectangle. Set pieces aside for use in Constructing Bag Body.

Quilting Outside Pockets

Note: The following instructions for the triangle units are known to quilters as flying geese units.

1. Draw a diagonal line on wrong side of each 2½-inch cream square (Figure 2).

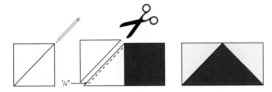

Figure 2

2. Place a 2½-inch cream square, right sides together with drawn diagonal line facing up, on the right side of a 2½ x 4½-inch brown rectangle. Sew on the diagonal line. Trim the seam allowance to ¼ inch, referring to Figure 2. Press toward cream.

3. Repeat on opposite side of brown rectangle to create a triangle unit, again referring to Figure 2.

4. Repeat steps 1–3 to make six triangle units.

5. Sew two triangle units together (Figure 3). Repeat to make two triangle sets.

Make 2

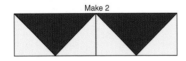

Figure 3

6. Sew a triangle set to one long edge of each 4½ x 8½-inch brown rectangle (Figure 4). Press seam toward brown piece. Repeat to make two outside side pockets.

Make 2   Make 2

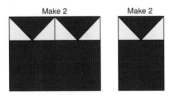

Figure 4

7. Sew a triangle unit to a 4½ x 4½-inch brown piece square, again referring to Figure 4. Press seam toward brown. Repeat to make two outside end pockets.

8. Layer and spray-baste together each 6½ x 8½-inch batting rectangle with an outside side pocket. Quilt following step 2 of Quilting Bag Body.

9. Repeat step 8 with the two 4½ x 6½-inch cotton batting rectangles and the two outside end pockets.

10. Sew a 6½ x 8½-inch brown rectangle to the top of an outside side pocket (Figure 5). Press brown rectangle to wrong side and topstitch, again referring to Figure 5. This creates the lining for the outside side pocket.

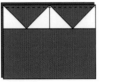

Figure 5

11. Repeat step 10 for remaining side pocket and for end pockets with 4½ x 6½-inch brown rectangles. Set aside for use in Constructing Bag Body.

Constructing Bag Body

1. Pin an outside side pocket to an orange quilted bag side rectangle matching side and bottom edges (Figure 6). Baste together ⅛ inch from raw edges. Repeat to make two bag side units and two bag end units, using quilted bag end rectangles with outside end pockets.

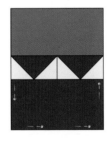

Figure 6   **Figure 7**

2. Match 10½-inch edges of quilted bag side unit and quilted bag end unit, referring to Figure 7. Sew units together beginning at bag top and stopping ¼ inch from bag bottom (Figure 7). Backstitch at beginning and end of seam to secure.

3. Sew bag side and end units together to make bag body, referring to Figure 8. Press seams open.

Figure 8

4. Pin and stitch bag body to quilted bag bottom, matching bag bottom corners to bag body seams (Figure 9). Turn right side out.

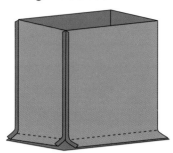

Figure 9

Bag Lining

1. To make lining pockets, sew two 6½ x 8½-inch cream rectangles together along 8½-inch edge. Press one rectangle to wrong side and topstitch. Repeat with all pocket pieces to make two each of 6½ x 8½-inch side pockets and 4½ x 6½-inch end pockets.

2. To construct bag lining, pin and stitch cream pockets and orange lining pieces together as in steps 1–3 of Constructing Bag Body, except, leave at least a 4-inch opening in one side seam for turning.

3. Pin and stitch lining to lining bottom, matching bottom corners to body seams, referring to Figure 9. *Do not turn right side out.*

Completing the Bag

1. Press 6½ x 24¼-inch brown strip in half lengthwise, wrong sides together.

2. Unfold and sew short ends of strip right sides together and press seam open. Refold along lengthwise crease and press to make bag top band.

3. Mark centers of end units of bag body. Pin top band to top of bag, matching top raw edges and band seam to one end unit center (Figure 10). Baste and set aside.

Figure 10

4. Fold and press a 5-inch x fabric width brown strip lengthwise, right sides together. Sew along the long edge. Turn right side out and press.

5. Repeat step 4 with each brown, cream and orange print 5-inch x fabric width strip to make two of each color.

6. Group together one each brown, cream and orange print strip and stitch together at one of the short ends, ⅛ inch from end (Figure 11).

Figure 11

7. Loosely braid strips together to make handle and secure ends with pin. Measure 31 inches from beginning end and stitch braid together as in step 6 to secure. Trim to ⅛-inch seam allowance. Press both ends only flat.

8. Repeat steps 6 and 7 to make a second loose braid 24½-inches long for embellishment.

9. Center and pin the ends of the 31-inch braid at center marks on ends of top bag band, referring to Figure 12.

Figure 12

10. Place bag inside lining, right sides together. Match top raw edges and seams. Pin and sew together.

11. Turn right side out through open lining side seam. Hand-stitch lining seam closed.

12. Place lining and handle into bag, pulling bag top band up (Figure 13). Press seam flat.

Figure 13

13. Edgestitch bag band close to the band top edge and the seam around the bag band. Topstitch ⅛ inch above first stitching on lower band.

14. Follow manufacturer's instructions for adding grommets. Center four grommets on band (two on front and back) 1 inch from bag side seams, referring to Figure 14.

Figure 14

15. Pin one end of the 24½-inch-long embellishment braid, made in step 8, to the band at the side seam (Figure 15). Thread free end of braid through the grommets, meeting the ends at the band seam. Pin.

Figure 15

16. Sew the ends to the band by machine-stitching through all thicknesses ⅛ inch on either side of the seam (Figure 16).

17. Turn bag top band down toward outside of bag and pull handle up to complete bag. ❖

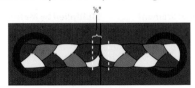

Figure 16

Meet the Designer

I simply love to design projects that make people smile. Even as a small child, I enjoyed making things out of paper, clay and fabric.

In 1989, I started Pearl Louise Designs and shortly after opened The Thimble Cottage Quilt Shop in Rapid City, S.D. (www.thimblecottage.com). My quilt shop has evolved over the years and customers come from near and far to enjoy our huge selection of fabrics, patterns and classes. I also design whimsical and home decor fabrics for Troy Corp.

Enjoy the variety of bags and purses and remember, "happiness is homemade."

Pearl Louise Krush

Metric Conversion Charts

Metric Conversions

Canada/U.S. Measurement				Multiplied by	Metric Measurement
yards	x	.9144	=		metres (m)
yards	x	91.44	=		centimetres (cm)
inches	x	2.54	=		centimetres (cm)
inches	x	25.40	=		millimetres (mm)
inches	x	.0254	=		metres (m)

Canada/U.S. Measurement				Multiplied by	Metric Measurement
centimetres	x	.3937	=		inches
metres	x	1.0936	=		yards

Standard Equivalents

Canada/U.S. Measurement		Metric Measurement			Canada/U.S. Measurement		Metric Measurement		
⅛ inch	=	3.20 mm	=	0.32 cm	1⅜ yards	=	125.73 cm	=	1.26 m
¼ inch	=	6.35 mm	=	0.635 cm	1½ yards	=	137.16 cm	=	1.37 m
⅜ inch	=	9.50 mm	=	0.95 cm	1⅝ yards	=	148.59 cm	=	1.49 m
½ inch	=	12.70 mm	=	1.27 cm	1¾ yards	=	160.02 cm	=	1.60 m
⅝ inch	=	15.90 mm	=	1.59 cm	1⅞ yards	=	171.44 cm	=	1.71 m
¾ inch	=	19.10 mm	=	1.91 cm	2 yards	=	182.88 cm	=	1.83 m
⅞ inch	=	22.20 mm	=	2.22 cm	2⅛ yards	=	194.31 cm	=	1.94 m
1 inch	=	25.40 mm	=	2.54 cm	2¼ yards	=	205.74 cm	=	2.06 m
⅛ yard	=	11.43 cm	=	0.11 m	2⅜ yards	=	217.17 cm	=	2.17 m
¼ yard	=	22.86 cm	=	0.23 m	2½ yards	=	228.60 cm	=	2.29 m
⅜ yard	=	34.29 cm	=	0.34 m	2⅝ yards	=	240.03 cm	=	2.40 m
½ yard	=	45.72 cm	=	0.46 m	2¾ yards	=	251.46 cm	=	2.51 m
⅝ yard	=	57.15 cm	=	0.57 m	2⅞ yards	=	262.88 cm	=	2.63 m
¾ yard	=	68.58 cm	=	0.69 m	3 yards	=	274.32 cm	=	2.74 m
⅞ yard	=	80.00 cm	=	0.80 m	3⅛ yards	=	285.75 cm	=	2.86 m
1 yard	=	91.44 cm	=	0.91 m	3¼ yards	=	297.18 cm	=	2.97 m
1⅛ yards	=	102.87 cm	=	1.03 m	3⅜ yards	=	308.61 cm	=	3.09 m
1¼ yards	=	114.30 cm	=	1.14 m	3½ yards	=	320.04 cm	=	3.20 m
					3⅝ yards	=	331.47 cm	=	3.31 m
					3¾ yards	=	342.90 cm	=	3.43 m
					3⅞ yards	=	354.32 cm	=	3.54 m
					4 yards	=	365.76 cm	=	3.66 m
					4⅛ yards	=	377.19 cm	=	3.77 m
					4¼ yards	=	388.62 cm	=	3.89 m
					4⅜ yards	=	400.05 cm	=	4.00 m
					4½ yards	=	411.48 cm	=	4.11 m
					4⅝ yards	=	422.91 cm	=	4.23 m
					4¾ yards	=	434.34 cm	=	4.34 m
					4⅞ yards	=	445.76 cm	=	4.46 m
					5 yards	=	457.20 cm	=	4.57 m

Purses, Bags & More is published by DRG, 306 East Parr Road, Berne, IN 46711. Printed in USA. Copyright © 2011 DRG. All rights reserved. This publication may not be reproduced in part or in whole without written permission from the publisher.

RETAIL STORES: If you would like to carry this pattern book or any other DRG publications, visit DRGwholesale.com

Every effort has been made to ensure that the instructions in this pattern book are complete and accurate. We cannot, however, take responsibility for human error, typographical mistakes or variations in individual work. Please visit ClotildeCustomerCare.com to check for pattern updates.

ISBN: 978-1-59217-316-7

1 2 3 4 5 6 7 8 9

HOUSE of WHITE BIRCHES
PUBLISHERS SINCE 1947

48

Photo Index

4

8

13

18

22

25

30

34

37

42